HURRICANES AND TWISTERS

By Robert Irving

Illustrated with Diagrams and Photographs
Line Illustrations by Ruth Adler

SCHOLASTIC BOOK SERVICES

Published by Scholastic Book Services, a division
of Scholastic Magazines, Inc., New York, N.Y.

Other books by Robert Irving

ROCKS AND MINERALS

ENERGY AND POWER

SOUND AND ULTRASONICS

Copyright 1955 by Irving Adler. This edition is published by Scholastic Book Services, a division of Scholastic Magazines, Inc., by arrangement with Alfred A. Knopf, Inc.

6th printing . . . . August 1967
Printed in the U.S.A.

CONTENTS

FOREWORD

Hurricanes and tornadoes are demonstrations of Mother Nature's dynamic displays of power. When they develop, they bring terrifying experiences to those who are unfortunate enough to be brought into direct contact with these demons of the air. The weather conditions which are necessary for the creation of these two types of storms are somewhat similar — essentially they need an abundance of warm and moist air in the lower layers of the atmosphere and cool and even dry air aloft in order to be born. It is under conditions such as these that the air becomes unstable and permits strong updrafts to be established to set the stage for a counter-clockwise, spirally inward and upward turning of the air to the extent that a full-fledged storm such as a hurricane may come into being.

These fantastic storms are interesting in many of their aspects — their very origin, their travel peculiarities, their size and shape, their tremendous force and power, and finally their dissipation or dying out. While meteorologists have learned something about the behavior of these storms, much more research is necessary before a complete understanding will result. We can only hope for success along this line, however, since the physical processes taking place in the atmosphere to produce weather are elusive and well hidden. But experience is a wonderful teacher. We learn something from each occurrence of a hurricane or a tornado, both from the point of view of forecasting and also discovering what to do to protect life and property when word is received that either one or the other is headed in our direction or is in the process of developing.

In this book, Robert Irving has brought out in an interesting fashion the highlights of hurricanes and tornadoes. The facts presented here will serve well to plant the seeds of knowledge in the minds of people so that they will be in a better position to take action when confronted with the threat of a hurricane or a tornado.

ERNEST J. CHRISTIE
Formerly, Head Meteorologist
U.S. Weather Bureau Office
New York, New York

To my daughter PEGGY,
who is proud to share her name with a hurricane

1. HAZEL WAS HERE

THE Manhattan end of the Queensboro Bridge in New York faces a row of stores on Second Avenue. People who drove off the bridge in October, 1954, saw the front of one of these stores covered with boards to close up a broken window. A big sign, painted across the boards in bright red letters, announced to the world that "Hazel Was Here!"

Hazel is not a publicity-seeking WAC, jealous of the fame the GI's won for Kilroy during World War II, when they left word all over Europe that "Kilroy Was Here." Hazel is of a different breed. People are happiest when she and her sisters are far, far away. Hazel is one of the hurricanes of 1954. The sign on the store front was a reminder that the broken window was one of many souvenirs she left in New York City when she passed by on her way to Canada.

HAZEL'S PRANKS

Smashing windows was only one of the milder pranks that Hazel played during her short but wild life. In the ten days that she lived she spread death and destruction wherever she went.

When she crossed the island of Haiti, in the West Indies, her winds blew the sea into the city of Jérémie. The water swept small buildings away and carried some of them out to sea. By the time Hazel was through with Haiti, very little of the city of Jérémie was left, and some inland villages were completely demolished. Hazel killed over one hundred people in Haiti alone.

When she reached the United States, she cut through eight states from South Carolina to New York. She brought with her high tides that invaded low areas on the coast and drove people out of their homes. Her winds blew the roofs off houses and

smashed buildings. They also blew down telephone and electric power lines. Her heavy rains caused floods that washed out roads and undermined bridges.

Where trees fell, they blocked roadways. Where power lines fell, large areas were left without electricity. Where water lines and sewers were broken, there was great danger of outbreaks of disease.

In Richmond, Virginia, Hazel broke a piece off the steeple of the Trinity Methodist Church. At the shipyard in Newport News, Virginia, she pulled the unfinished battleship *Kentucky* loose and washed it up on shore. In Paterson, New Jersey, she blew a trap door off the roof of a church. Her winds sucked the air out of the church and formed a vacuum inside. This made one of the walls collapse, showering bricks on top of the people assembled in the church.

On a Delaware farm, she blew over a 230-foot brooding house containing thousands of four-day-old baby chicks. The farmer and his family worked through the night, by candlelight and the light of his automobile headlights, trying desperately to save some of the chicks.

Wherever Hazel went people were killed. In North Carolina a boy was killed by a falling tree. In Maryland a man was killed when a brick wall fell on him. In Delaware a woman was killed when the wind blew her in front of a trolley bus. In Pennsylvania a bus driver was electrocuted when he tried to remove a fallen wire from the top of his bus. In New York a woman was killed by a sign that was blown off a building. In Virginia four seamen were drowned when a tugboat sank. Hazel was responsible for thirty-nine deaths in the United States.

GETTING OUT OF HAZEL'S WAY

In some places, where people knew in time that Hazel was coming, they were able to get out of her way. By moving themselves or their property out of danger zones, they reduced the damage that she did.

In Washington, D.C., when word came that Hazel was on her way, the schools sent their pupils home, and federal offices were closed. So most people were at home, instead of being out on the street, when Hazel came roaring through.

In South Carolina and North Carolina, people who lived on the beaches were warned that extra-high tides were coming that would flood the shore. Thousands of people left their homes to escape the rising tides.

In Virginia, eighty large naval ships were sent to sea to ride out the storm. In New Jersey, Delaware, Massachusetts, and Rhode Island, there was danger that Army and Navy planes might be damaged by the high winds expected at the airfields. So the planes were flown to other airports where they could sit out the storm in safety. Many went to Albany, Buffalo,

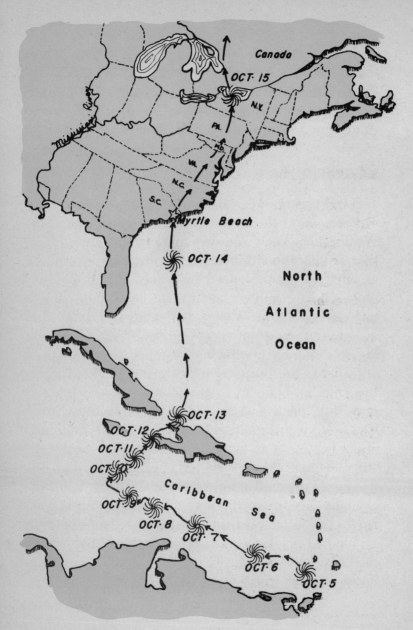

OCT. 15

Canada

N.Y.

PA.

MD.

VA.

N.C.

S.C.

Myrtle Beach

OCT. 14

North

Atlantic

Ocean

OCT. 13

OCT. 12

OCT. 11

OCT.

OCT. 9

OCT. 8

Caribbean Sea

OCT. 7

OCT. 6

OCT. 5

and Schenectady, in New York. Seven Navy seaplanes that flew from Norfolk, Virginia, to Corpus Christi, Texas, ran into another storm there. They were stranded in rough water out in the bay, and had to be dropped food from a helicopter.

BIOGRAPHY OF HAZEL

Hazel was born on October 5, 1954, near the island of Grenada, at the eastern end of the Caribbean Sea. Weathermen knew she was there when reports from that neighborhood showed a drop in air pressure and an increase in the speed of winds. She grew very quickly. By October eighth she was big enough to be described as "a very dangerous storm." Within a hundred miles of her center, winds were one hundred and twenty-five miles an hour. Two hundred miles from the center, winds were as high as forty-five miles an hour. At first, although she was big and powerful, she was lazy. For four days she drifted slowly westward into the Caribbean Sea, moving only about five miles an hour. Then she turned north, and still moving slowly, crossed over Haiti into the Atlantic Ocean. There, on October thirteenth, she changed her pace. Turning to the northwest, she began to race toward the coast of the United States, at a speed of about forty miles an hour. She struck the coast at Myrtle Beach, South Carolina, and then raced on over North Carolina, Virginia, Washington,

D.C., Maryland, Pennsylvania, and New York. On October fifteenth she crossed Lake Ontario into Canada. After that the Weather Bureau considered her an ordinary inland storm, so Hazel, the hurricane, was declared officially dead ten days after she was born. But her ghost carried on with enough strength to kill eighty-five people in Canada.

HAZEL WAS DIFFERENT

From the time that she was born, the people of the Weather Bureau kept their eyes on Hazel. They tried to figure out which way she would go so they could warn people in her path. But Hazel made things difficult for them in many ways. Instead of moving slowly all the time the way a well-behaved hurricane should, she suddenly picked up speed when she was eight days old. Instead of veering east the way northward-moving hurricanes usually do, she veered to the west. Instead of growing rapidly weaker after she left the ocean, she remained strong until she reached Canada.

Hazel was also different in another way. She was the third hurricane to strike the east coast of the United States in 1954. She was preceded by Edna, who struck the New England states, and by Carol, who swept over Long Island and New England. It is unusual for even one hurricane a year to strike inland so far north. Nobody expected three to do it in the same year.

HAZEL'S SISTERS

Hazel was the eighth 1954 hurricane born in the Caribbean Sea or in the Atlantic Ocean. The first of the year was Alice, who struck Mexico on June twenty-fifth. The second, Barbara, stayed in the Caribbean Sea, and died July thirtieth without doing any great harm. The third was Carol, who came north, and moved across Long Island and New England on August thirty-first. She killed sixty-eight people and destroyed property worth five hundred million dollars. In September, Dolly, the fourth hurricane, moved north over the Atlantic Ocean, but kept away from shore. Then came Edna, following about the same path as Carol. She barely missed Long Island, and killed eleven people in New England. Florence, who came next, crossed the Gulf of Mexico and did slight damage in Mexico and Texas. Later, Gilda trailed after Florence as September drew to a close. Then Hazel came. Carol, Edna and Hazel together killed over three hundred people, and did damage worth $1,355,000,000.

HAZEL'S COUSINS

The hurricanes of the Caribbean Sea, the Gulf of Mexico, and the North Atlantic Ocean are part of a larger family of storms called *tropical cyclones*. They all start over the sea near the equator. They form over all tropical oceans except the South Atlantic. They are found under many names in different parts of the world. In the western part of the North Pacific Ocean, near China, Formosa and Japan, they are called *typhoons*. In the Bay of Bengal and the northern Indian Ocean they are called *cyclones*. In Australia they are called *willy-willies*. In the Philippine Islands they are called *baguios* (pronounced bah-gyoz). At the Cape of Good Hope they are called *trovados*. On the west coast of Central America they are called *papagallos*.

The word hurricane comes from the name *Hunrakan*, the god of stormy weather of the Indians of Guatemala, a small country on the Caribbean Sea. The word cyclone means "coil of a snake." It was first used by Henry Piddington, president of the Marine Courts at Calcutta, India, in the middle of the nineteenth century, because the winding whirlwinds of a cyclone resemble the coils of a snake. The word typhoon may have come from the Chinese *ta feng*, meaning "big wind."

2. HOW THE HURRICANES GOT THEIR NAMES

IN some ways a hurricane is like a person. After it is born, it grows and develops, then becomes old and dies. Each hurricane has a character of its own. There are big ones and little ones, fast ones and slow ones. Each follows its own path through the world, and people remember it long after it is gone. So it seems natural to give hurricanes names, and to talk about them almost as if they were alive.

HURRICANES WITH SAINTS' NAMES

The first people to give names to hurricanes were those who knew them best, the people of Puerto Rico. Their small island country is in the West Indies, the chain of islands that stretches from

Florida to Venezuela. Many hurricanes pass near Puerto Rico, and some of them cross the island as they move up north toward the coast of Florida. The people of Puerto Rico expect some of these unwelcome visitors every year. Each one that comes is named after the saint's day on which it arrives. The hurricane of July 26, 1825, which blew down seven thousand houses and killed three hundred and seventy-four people, was called the Santa Ana. The hurricane of August 8, 1899, which killed three thousand people, was called the San Ciriaco.

THE HURRICANE THAT CAME TO A FUNERAL

In the nearby island of Hispaniola, one hurricane got its name in a different way. On September 23, 1834, the people of Santo Domingo came to church for the funeral of the priest Padre Ruiz (Father Ruiz). During the services, a hurricane struck the island. It tore up trees, blew down houses, sank ships and killed many people. Ever since this terrible day, the people of Santo Domingo have called that hurricane the "Padre Ruiz," after the poor priest whose funeral was spoiled.

MARIA, THE STORYBOOK STORM

Things that happen in real life sometimes find their way into storybooks. But sometimes it works the

11

other way 'round: something in a story finds its way into real life. Giving girls' names to hurricanes started in this way. It all began with a story called "Storm," written by George Stewart in 1941. In this story the author describes how a weatherman recognized the first signs that a storm was being born over the Pacific Ocean. The weatherman used to amuse himself by naming storms after girls that he knew. He named this one "Maria." The author then describes how Maria grew and developed, and how she changed the lives of people when she struck the west coast of the United States.

HUNTING TYPHOONS IN THE PACIFIC

During World War II the weathermen of the U.S. Army and U.S. Navy had to study weather conditions over the Pacific Ocean. One of their duties was to warn American ships and planes when a typhoon was coming. Like the hero of George Stewart's book, whenever they spotted a typhoon they gave it a girl's name. The first one of the year was given a name beginning with A. The second one got a name beginning with B. They used all the letters from A to W, and still the typhoons kept coming. They had to use three lists from A to W to have enough names to go around! This was the first list of hurricane names that followed the alphabet. It served as a model for the system the Weather Bureau introduced later, in 1952.

THREE IS A CROWD

The hurricanes that sometimes strike the east coast of the United States all begin near the West Indies. Before 1950, the Weather Bureau had no special system for tagging them. When a hurricane was born, the Weather Bureau collected information about it, so it could tell how fast it was moving and where it would go next. Weather reports warned people in the path of the hurricane, so they might do what they could to protect themselves. This system worked out fine as long as weather reports talked about only one hurricane at a time. But one week in September, 1950, there were three hurricanes in the Caribbean Sea at the same time. Then things began to get confused. Some people got the hurricanes mixed up, and didn't know which was which. This convinced the Weather Bureau that it needed a code for naming the hurricanes, in order to avoid confusion in the future.

In 1951, a conference of weathermen decided to tag hurricanes with the letters of the alphabet. For radio messages, each letter was to be sent out as a word, using the Army alphabet code: Able, Baker, Charlie, Dog, Easy, etc. But then they found that foreign weather stations in the Caribbean had just agreed to use other code words for the letters of the alphabet: Alpha, Bravo, Coca, Delta, Echo, Foxtrot, etc. So things were mixed up again. The next year the weathermen decided to solve the problem by giving each hurricane a name of its own, taken from a fixed list in alphabetical order. So, from 1952 to 1954, the hurricanes of each year were named from this list: Alice, Barbara, Carol, Dolly, Edna, Florence, Gilda, Hazel, Irene, Jill, Katherine, Lucy, Mabel, Norma, Orpha, Patsy, Queen, Rachel, Susie, Tina, Una, Vicky and Wallis.

THE OFFICE GIRL AND THE DUCHESS

When the newspapers and radio followed the travels of hurricane Hazel, and described the damage she did, girls named Hazel were probably in for a little teasing by their friends. To shield itself from the anger of offended Hazels, as well as Alices, Barbaras, Carols and others, all over the country, the Weather Bureau may say: "Any resemblance between hurricane names and the names of particular girls is purely coincidental." And really, it is. Only two of the names may have been picked with particular girls in mind. The name Orpha, it is reported, was taken from one of the girls working in a Weather Bureau office. And Wallis is a name made famous by the Duchess of Windsor, the woman for whom a king of England gave up his throne.

HURRICANES OF 1955

In 1954, some women were angry because hurricanes were given their names, and they complained to the Weather Bureau. But many other women were proud to see their names make headlines, even as the names of destructive storms. In spite of the protests it received, and because there were many more more favorable comments than criticisms, the Weather Bureau decided to continue using girls' names for hurricanes. It issued a new list for 1955. These were the names that the Weather Bureau picked: Alice, Brenda, Connie, Diane, Edith, Flora, Gladys, Hilda, Ione, Janet, Katie, Linda, Martha, Nelly, Orva, Peggy, Queena, Rosa, Stella, Trudy, Ursa, Verna, Wilma, Xena, Yvonne and Zelda.

3. THE POWER AND FURY
OF HURRICANES

MOST POWERFUL STORM

THE United States produces more electric power than any other country. All of its electric generators together can produce about one hundred and fifty million horsepower. Although this amount is big, it is tiny compared to the power of a single hurricane. One full-grown hurricane can produce five hundred million million horsepower. This is over three million times as much as the power produced by all the electric generators in the United States .put together. So it is not surprising that a hurricane is considered the most powerful and destructive kind of storm.

MORE POWER THAN THE H-BOMB

Today, when we think of great destructive power, we think of the atomic bomb and the hydrogen bomb. One atomic bomb dropped on the Japanese city of Hiroshima in 1945 destroyed everything in a circle two miles wide, and killed about ninety thousand people. A hydrogen bomb is the giant of the atomic bomb family. One hydrogen bomb may be as powerful as one thousand atomic bombs, and could destroy everything in a circle twenty miles wide. But, although it is a giant, the hydrogen bomb is a pigmy compared to a hurricane. To match the power of a hurricane it would be necessary to explode several thousand atomic bombs *each second* for as long as the hurricane rages. And most hurricanes last well over a week. Fortunately, the power of a hurricane isn't packed into a small space like an A-bomb or an H-bomb. It is spread out over about half a million square miles on the ground, and seven or eight miles in the air. This thins out the power of the hurricane and usually prevents it from doing as much damage in any one place as was done by the bomb that fell on Hiroshima.

BIG WIND

The power of a hurricane is in its winds. Hurricane winds are often one hundred miles an hour, and sometimes much higher. During the 1938 hurricane that struck the New England states, one weather station measured a wind of one hundred and eighty-six miles an hour. Winds that travel that fast push with tremendous force against anything that stands in their way. A wind of fifty miles an hour pushes with a force of ten pounds on every square foot it strikes. A wind of one hundred miles an hour pushes with a force that is four times as great. A wind of one hundred and fifty miles an hour exerts a force nine times as great, or ninety pounds on every square foot. If a thirteen-year-old boy of average height and weight were caught in a wind of one hundred and fifty miles an hour, the wind would push him with a force of about five hundred pounds. It would blow him around like a piece of paper! The same wind, blowing against a tree whose trunk is two feet wide and thirty feet high, would push with a force of almost three tons against the trunk alone. The full force against the trunk and branches together might be from five to eight tons. That's why a hurricane wind can pull trees up out of the ground, roots and all, and topple them over like dominoes. If a wind of one hundred and fifty miles an hour blows against a wall forty feet long and three stories high, it pushes it with a force of forty-five tons. That's why a hurricane wind can smash buildings and tear off roofs.

STONES THAT FLY

Almost two hundred years ago, the people of France were surprised to see the first lighter-than-air balloon sail across the sky. But today, flying is such a common sight, it doesn't surprise us any more. We don't think it unusual to see a heavier-than-air airplane, built of metal, glide through the air as easily as a feather in the wind. But even we would be startled to see great solid blocks of stone or lead sail through the air on the wind. Yet this has actually happened. In August, 1930, a hurricane struck Great Abaco Island, one of the Bahama Islands that lie east of Florida. The winds in this hurricane were above two hundred miles an hour. The storm tore down two churches built of heavy stone three feet thick. Some of the stone blocks were carried by the wind a distance of half a mile. About a hundred years earlier, in 1831, a hurricane wind performed a similar feat of strength at Barbados. This is one of the islands that stretch from Puerto Rico to Venezuela. The wind lifted a piece of lead weighing four hundred pounds, and carried it over a third of a mile away.

A WIND-DRIVEN SPEAR

A stone blown by a hurricane wind is like a cannon ball. A simple stick sailing with a strong wind can become a deadly spear or javelin. On September 13, 1928, the hurricane San Felipe swept across the island of Puerto Rico. Among the many things the wind lifted off the ground was a pine board ten feet long, three inches wide and one inch thick. The wind drove this board right through the trunk of a palm tree as if the tree were as soft as butter. The tree, pierced by the board, is shown in the photographic section following page 81.

A GIANT BULLDOZER

A bulldozer is a powerful engine that pushes a broad metal shield across the ground. If it meets any obstacles in its path it butts them stubbornly like an angry goat, and pushes them aside. It can invade a field overgrown with trees and shrubs and strip it bare, leaving it clean and level enough to serve as an airfield. A hurricane that crosses cultivated fields can act like a giant bulldozer. The wind may strip off every plant, leaving the ground completely bare. So even in the open country, where there are few houses to smash or trees to uproot, hurricane winds can do great damage.

THE STORM WAVE

All hurricanes, and their cousins of the tropical cyclone family, are born over the sea. While they are still over the sea, their winds transfer part of their power to the water under them. The winds blow against the water, and push it before them, forming a storm wave. When the wave approaches an island or continent, it is forced up onto the shore and floods the land. If the wave is driven into a bay, it is trapped there. As it climbs the underwater slope of the shore, it mounts higher and higher to form a giant wall of water that sweeps across the land. In 1938, when a hurricane struck New England, in some places the storm wave rose twenty-five feet. Storm waves in other parts of the world have been as high as forty feet. The storm wave is the deadliest part of a hurricane. More than three-fourths of all the deaths caused by hurricanes and other tropical cyclones are the result of storm waves that invade the land.

SHIPS ON SHORE, HOUSES AT SEA

When a storm wave sweeps onto the land, it sometimes carries ships inland with it. Later, when the water pulls back to the sea, it may leave the ships stranded, high and dry, on the shore. A ship was left on a railroad track alongside a wrecked train in New England by the hurricane of September, 1938.

When the water flows back to the sea, while it leaves ships on shore, it may carry houses out to sea with it. When Hazel roared across Haiti in October,

1954, the storm wave flooded the city of Jérémie. When the water pulled back, many homes were washed into the sea.

ISLANDS DISAPPEAR

There are islands just off the coast near Charleston, South Carolina, and near Savannah, Georgia. On August 27, 1893, some of these islands disappeared from view when the sea rose during a hurricane. When the water fell back again, it was found that one thousand people had been killed on the islands. On November 9, 1932, a storm wave invaded the city of Santa Cruz del Sur, in Cuba. Two thousand five hundred people, out of a population of four thousand, died that day.

THE HOOGHLY RIVER DISASTER

The worst storm wave of history is the one that rolled up the mouth of the Hooghly River in India on October 7, 1737. The Hooghly River empties into the Bay of Bengal, which lies east of the Indian peninsula. The Bay of Bengal is the favorite haunt of the Bengal cyclones. When the cyclones whirl in toward shore, they build up storm waves of great height. On October 7, 1737, the storm wave rose forty feet high. When it struck the shore, what was once dry land became the bottom of a raging sea. This wave alone killed three hundred thousand people, more than three times as many as were killed by the atom bomb at Hiroshima. Only one other storm wave in recent history was as destructive as this one. In 1881, a storm wave built up by a typhoon in the South China Sea killed three hundred thousand people when it struck the coast at Haiphong.

REPEAT PERFORMANCE

Storm waves have come back again and again to spread tragedy over the shores of the Bay of Bengal. As if the slaughter of 1737 were not enough, a storm wave swept up the mouth of the Hooghly River again in 1864. This time fifty thousand people were drowned. The flood also caused an outbreak of disease that killed another thirty thousand people. Twelve years later another great storm wave rolled across Backergunge, east of the mouth of the Hooghly River. This wave drowned one hundred thousand people. Epidemics that followed the flood killed one hundred thousand more. Then, in 1885, a storm wave twenty-two feet high swept over False Point Harbor, west of the mouth of the Hooghly River. The water covered up whole villages and carried away people, houses and cattle.

A TOWN IS BURIED

A Bay of Bengal storm wave once buried a whole town with all its twenty thousand inhabitants. The town, called Coringa, was on the western shore of the bay. In December, 1789, three giant waves rolled in from the sea, one after the other. The first one brought several feet of water into the town. The

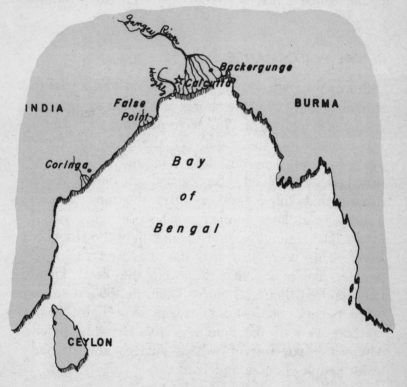

Home of the Bengal Cyclones

second one spread the water to the surrounding countryside. The third one completely covered everything in that neighborhood. When the water withdrew, the town of Coringa was gone. It was completely buried under sand and mud that had settled out of the water. A second layer of sand and mud was piled on top of this one when another storm wave flooded the same area fifty years later.

STORM CURRENTS

Besides launching storm waves, the whirling winds of a hurricane also set up whirling currents in the water under them. The strength of these currents can be seen from what one of them did during a hurricane in August, 1915. A buoy weighing twenty-one thousand pounds was anchored in forty-two feet of water off the coast of Texas. The anchor weighed six thousand five hundred pounds, and the anchor chain, two hundred and fifty-two feet long, weighed three thousand two hundred and fifty pounds. A current set up by the hurricane tugged and tugged at the buoy, and carried it, dragging chain, anchor and all, a distance of ten miles.

TONS OF WATER FROM THE SKY

The winds of a hurricane carry thick clouds on their backs. Near the center of the storm the clouds reach down close to the ground, and reach up into the air to a height of eight miles. Out of these clouds, tons and tons of water pour down in torrents of rain. Sometimes as much rain will fall in a hurricane in one day as some rainy cities get in a whole year.

San Francisco is a city that gets a fair amount of rain brought in from the Pacific Ocean. If all the rain that fell on San Francisco in one year stayed where it fell, it would make a pool twenty-two inches deep. Paris, also a rainy city, gets twenty-one inches of rain a year. London gets twenty-five inches a year; Chicago gets thirty-three inches a year. But at Adjuntas, Puerto Rico, during the hurricane of September 13, 1928, twenty-nine and six-tenths inches of rain fell in *one day*.

The greatest amount of rain that ever fell in twenty-four hours poured down on the city of Baguio in the Philippine Islands, during a *baguio* in July, 1911. The twenty-four-hour rainfall was forty-six inches. This is more than the amount of rain that falls on San Francisco in two years! The total rainfall in that storm was eighty-eight inches in four days, or as much as San Francisco gets in four years.

A hurricane once brought Silver Hill, Jamaica, ninety-six and five-tenths inches of rain in four days. A typhoon in July, 1913, dropped eighty-one and five-tenths inches in three days on Funkiko, Formosa.

Heavy rains like these, falling on a farmer's fields

in a few days, would smash his crops to a pulp. One inch of rainfall on an acre contains one hundred and thirteen tons of water. The eighty-eight-inch rainfall at Baguio battered the countryside with almost ten thousand tons of water on each acre.

One of the worst hurricanes that ever struck the island of Puerto Rico was the San Ciriaco in 1899. This storm moved across the whole length of the island. It dropped over two and one-half billion tons of rain on Puerto Rico alone. The heavy rain, the winds of ninety miles an hour, and a storm wave combined to kill over three thousand people, and destroy property worth twenty million dollars.

INLAND FLOODS

When rain reaches the ground, it doesn't stay where it falls. Some of it soaks into the ground and some runs downhill. When the rainfall is heavy, the ground is soon filled with all it can hold, and then all the rest runs downhill to form big pools where the ground is low. So the heavy rains of a hurricane always cause inland floods. Whenever a hurricane strikes a city, the newspapers the next day are full of pictures of streets that look like lakes, with automobiles stranded in deep water. But some floods have done far worse than halt automobile traffic. In September, 1921, a hurricane flood in San Antonio, Texas, filled some streets with water up to nine feet above the street level. The water rushed into hotels, theaters and stores on the ground floor. Fifty-one people were killed by the flood. Property damage amounted to five million dollars.

In June, 1934, during a hurricane, the rain came down in torrents on the Central American country of Honduras. As the water ran off into the streams, the streams rose higher and higher. The people of Pimienta, on the banks of the Ulua River, sought safety on top of a small hill. But the swirling water of the river surrounded the hill and steadily climbed up the slope. The river rose a full forty-five feet, covered the hill and drowned them all.

LANDSLIDES

When rain falls on a mountainside, the surface water soon starts flowing down the slope. First the raindrops collect to form puddles. From the puddles little fingers of water reach out, and then grow into small streams. The streams pick up bits of earth and carry them along down the slope. The small streams join to make larger streams, which then spread out to form sheets of flowing water. When the water reaches a stone, it flows around it on both sides, carrying away the earth that surrounds the stone. After the earth that held the stone in place is gone, the stone, pulled by its own weight, starts rolling down the slope, picking up speed as it goes.

Some of the rain water soaks into the ground, and then, while below the surface, starts seeping down the slope. When the rain is heavy, the underground seeping becomes a steady flow. The earth is loosened, and pulled by its own weight, it may slide down the slope on the back of the flowing underground streams. In this way some hurricane rains have launched landslides of rolling stones and sliding earth. Tons of earth and stone go roaring down the mountainside, and pile up at the foot of the slope. In El Salvador, tiny neighbor of Honduras, during the hurricane of June, 1934, whole towns were destroyed by landslides started by the heavy rainfall.

EARTHQUAKES IN A HURRICANE

Sometimes the damage done by a hurricane is made worse by an earthquake taking place at the same time. This happened on September 1, 1923, when a typhoon struck Japan. The earthquake shook the city of Tokyo, toppling houses and starting fires. The heaving earth also launched a *tsunami*, a giant wave that swept in from the ocean. The combined action of wind, quake, wave and fire destroyed almost all of Tokyo and all towns within forty miles. One hundred thousand people were killed that day.

The earthquake came at the same time as the typhoon. This may have been an accident. But it is also possible that the earthquake came *because of* the typhoon, which put unusual strains on the sea bottom near Japan. The sea bottom usually has a great weight pressing down on it. This is the combined weight of the water that lies over the sea bottom, and the air that lies over the sea. In a typhoon this weight is changed in two ways. Where the air pressure falls, at the center of the storm, there is less weight than usual pressing down on the sea bottom. Where a storm wave builds up, there is more weight than usual pressing down on the sea bottom. These changes in the weight that the sea bottom had to carry set up strains that may have caused the earth to heave.

NO ILL WIND

An old proverb says: It is an ill wind that blows nobody good. This proverb puts into words what people had noticed during centuries of experience. When something bad happens, it isn't always bad for everybody. In fact, some people may benefit from it. In the rare case where nobody at all benefits, it is an "ill wind" indeed. Hurricanes are bad winds that cause death and destruction. But bad as they are, no hurricane is the "ill wind" of the proverb, because even a hurricane does some people good. Places on the fringe of the storm, that are not struck by its full force, get the rain but not the destruction. And in those places the rain helps the crops grow.

In fact, because of a hurricane, a part of the state of Louisiana once got an *extra* crop. In September, 1772, a hurricane passed close by. The warmth and rain that it brought to this area made the trees blossom and bear fruit a second time that year.

FAMOUS HURRICANES

Some tropical cyclones are especially well known because they did unusually great damage, or they caused strange things to happen. Some of these have already been described in this chapter. One that will be remembered for a long time in the United States is the hurricane of September 21, 1938. After first wandering north over the Atlantic Ocean, it veered west and smashed its way across Long Island and New England. It killed six hundred people, and destroyed property worth three hundred and thirty million dollars.

Three years earlier the "Labor Day Hurricane" of 1935 brought tragedy to the low islands off the coast of Florida, the Florida Keys. That was one of the years of the great depression when many factories were closed and millions of people were out of work. Among them were seven hundred veterans of World War I who were settled in a government relief camp on the Keys, when the islands were struck by a furious hurricane. A rescue train that tried to reach them from the mainland was swept off the tracks by the storm. About four hundred people were killed.

A storm that Texas will never forget is the one that sent a storm wave into Galveston in September, 1900. The flood killed over six thousand people.

Human beings are not the only victims of hurricanes. We have a reminder of this fact in what happened on November 6, 1932. The S.S. *Phemius* was caught in a hurricane out at sea. Winds were over two hundred miles an hour. Hundreds of birds, trying to escape from the storm, settled on the ship. After a few hours they were all dead.

BARON MUNCHAUSEN AT SEA

The Adventures of Baron Munchausen is a famous book of tall tales that has amused people all over the world. In one of the stories in this book the Baron tells of riding on his horse through Poland in the wintertime. The countryside was covered with snow. It was night, and no village seemed to be near. The Baron stopped riding, tied his horse to what looked like the stump of a tree, and went to sleep on the ground. When he awoke in the daytime, he found himself in a churchyard. His horse was hanging above him, tied to the church steeple. The village had been buried by the snow the night before, and the "tree stump" to which he had tied his horse was really the steeple of the buried church.

During the night the weather had changed. When the snow melted, it left him lying in the churchyard, and left his horse hanging in the air.

A report of a hurricane that took place in 1759 sounds like one of Baron Munchausen's adventures. The good ship *Litbury* was caught by the storm near

some islands in the Gulf of Mexico. The captain of the ship cast anchor in what he thought was Hawke Channel. When he looked out of his cabin the next morning, the storm was over. The ship was high and dry on Elliott's Island, and the anchor was hanging from a branch of a nearby tree. During the storm the water had covered the island above the level of the highest trees. When the captain had cast anchor, the ship was over the island, and not in the channel as he had thought. When the water pulled back from the island, the ship was left on shore.

THE LOOP HURRICANE

One hurricane made itself famous in 1910 by making a loop in its path. After moving north over Cuba from the Caribbean Sea, it stopped, swung left to make a small loop, and crossed over Cuba again. Then it continued its journey north, moving across Florida and then up the coast of the United States to Cape Hatteras. After that it moved out into the Atlantic Ocean.

STORM . . . . HEADING THIS WAY . . . . .

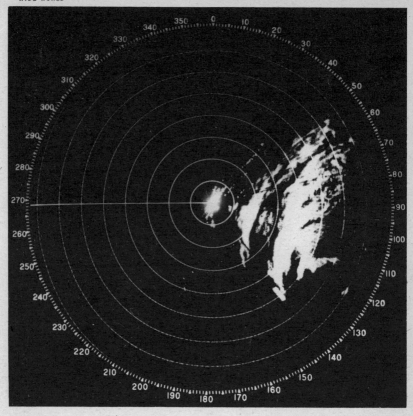

PICTURE OF DAISY ON RADARSCOPE: In 1958 for the first time a hurricane was tracked by radar all the way up the Atlantic coast—from its first appearance off Florida to its last gusts off New England. Men tracking a storm on the radarscope can actually see the arrangement of the clouds in a hurricane many miles away.

HANGING ON: Men and a tree bow before the winds of Hurricane Carol in Massachusetts. Carol began as a slow-moving hurricane, traveling only three hundred miles in three days. Then suddenly it raced up the coast, covering four hundred miles in twelve hours. (August 31, 1954.)

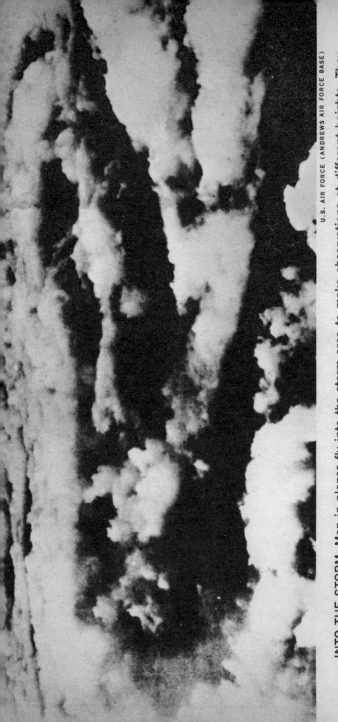

INTO THE STORM: Men in planes fly into the storm area to make observations at different heights. They record the temperature, pressure and moisture in the eye of each hurricane and in the upper air that surrounds it. Here they have photographed the circular pattern of tropical storm clouds.

THE SEA POURS IN: Extra-high tides brought by Hurricane Carol lash at a New England yacht club and rip the hurricane signal flag to tatters. (August 31, 1954.)

U.S. WEATHER BUREAU

FIRST PHOTOGRAPH: The first picture ever taken of a tornado was photographed in South Dakota in 1884.

TWISTER: A tornado begins with a funnel-shaped cloud that forms high in the air and then roars down to the ground. This twister raged through Detroit, Michigan. (June 16, 1946.)

CAROL TOPPLES STEEPLE: For the second time since 1804, a hurricane destroys a famous steeple. This is the steeple of Boston's Old North Church, where the lanterns were hung to tell Paul Revere how the British were coming. (September 1, 1954.)

4. THE HURRICANE SEASON

TEMPEST IN A BIG TEAPOT

IF you heat water in a teapot over a gas burner, as the water gets hot it warms the air above it. After a while, the water begins to boil. The bubbles that rise out of the water contain water vapor or steam. The steam mixes with the air above the water, and the mixture rises from the teapot. The rising mixture of air and steam sometimes pushes up the lid of the teapot. When the lid falls again, it strikes against the pot and makes a sound. Meanwhile, the bubbles bursting out of the water make the surface of the water jump around angrily, as if it were tossed about by a storm. The clatter of the lid and the bubbling of the water combine to make the storm in the teapot a noisy one. But the

The Big Teapot

noise and the restless dancing of the water can be stopped as easily as they were started. All you have to do is turn off the gas, and the storm in the teapot ends. When people get into an excited argument about something of no importance, and the argument can end as easily as it began, the argument reminds us of the imitation storm in the teapot, so we say they started "a tempest in a teapot."

But it isn't only imitation storms that look like the "tempest in a teapot." Real ones, such as hurricanes, do, too. A hurricane is a real tempest in a big teapot. It, too, is started by the heating of water. The water is in the biggest teapot of all, the sea. There is no gas burner heating the sea from below, but there is sunlight heating it from above. The heated sea water warms the air above it, just as the water in a teapot does. The sea doesn't boil, but some of the water at the surface does evaporate. This puts water vapor into the air, and makes the air wet. The warm, wet air is lighter than cool, dry air, so it begins to rise. This rising stream of air is sometimes the birthplace of a hurricane. Unlike a tempest in a teapot, it cannot be stopped by turning off the heat.

WHERE THE SUN SHINES MOST

Hurricanes begin where the sea is warmest. The sea is warmest where it gets the most sunlight. This happens near the equator, halfway between the North Pole and the South Pole. Places near the equator get more sunlight than other parts of the earth because the earth is round. To see why this is so, look at diagram A on page 48. This shows how sunlight streams in toward the earth in the spring or fall. The shaded parts show equal amounts of sunlight. The part striking the earth at the equator

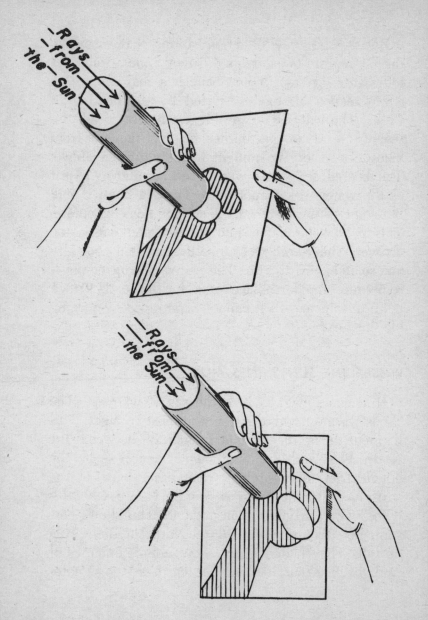

comes straight down from overhead. The part coming in near the North Pole strikes the ground at a slant. But the ground is warmed more by rays coming from overhead than by slanting rays. To see why, take a hollow tube and point it at the sun. Hold a piece of paper straight across under the mouth of the tube. The bundle of sunlight that comes through the tube will fall on the paper in a small circle surrounded by the shadow of the tube. This is like light coming from overhead. Now tilt the paper so that the light strikes it at a slant. The light that comes through the tube will now strike the paper in an oval-shaped space larger than the circle. Since the same amount of light has been spread out over a larger space, each part of the space gets less light than it got before. Since it gets less of the sun's rays, it will be warmed up less. Diagram A shows how the sunlight that falls near the pole is spread out over more ground than at the equator. Near the pole, where the sunlight is spread out over more ground, each part of the ground gets a smaller share of it. At the equator, where the same amount of sunlight is spread out over less ground, each part of the ground gets a larger share.

Rays that come to the ground at a slant also pass through more air before they reach the ground than rays that come from overhead. As a result, more of them are scattered or reflected away from the ground by the air, dust and clouds. This is another reason

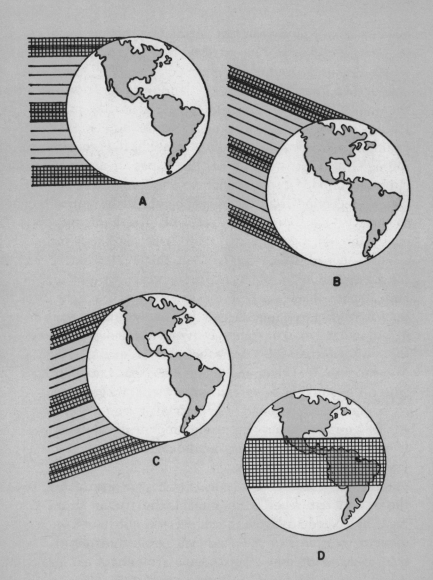

A

B

C

D

why slanting rays warm the ground less than rays that come from overhead. Both reasons together explain why sunlight in the spring and fall is strongest at the equator.

Diagram B shows how sunlight streams toward the earth around June twenty-first, when the sun is farthest north. Then the sunlight is strongest at places about one-fourth of the way between the equator and the North Pole. Diagram C shows how sunlight streams toward the earth around December twenty-first, when the sun is farthest south. Then the sunlight is strongest at places about one-fourth of the way between the equator and the South Pole. As the seasons change, the strongest sunlight moves back and forth between these two positions, so it is always in the narrow belt near the equator shown in diagram D. It is in this belt that hurricanes and other tropical cyclones are born.

HURRICANE CRADLES

The hurricanes that sometimes strike the east coast of the United States belong to two separate families. Each family comes from a different place. One of them is the Cape Verde family. The hurricanes in this family are born over the Atlantic Ocean near the Cape Verde Islands. These islands are near the coast of West Africa, directly east of the Caribbean Sea. Hurricanes that start there travel along a big circle around the North Atlantic Ocean. First they move west, then they swing north, and finally they head east again.

The Atlantic Ocean is separated from the Caribbean Sea by a chain of islands, arranged like steppingstones from South America to Florida. The Cape Verde hurricanes, as they circle around the ocean,

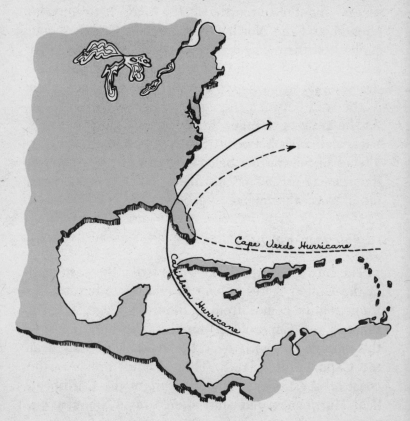

often pass right over these islands. Sometimes they strike the coast of the United States before heading east over the ocean again. One out of every three Cape Verde hurricanes will usually reach the coast.

The other family of hurricanes is the Caribbean family. They are usually born over the western part of the Caribbean Sea, near Central America. They usually travel northwest first, into the Gulf of Mexico. Then they swing northeast, sometimes crossing over Florida on their way to the Atlantic Ocean.

THE HURRICANE SEASON

Hurricanes are born *where* the sea is warmest. Most of them are born *when* it is warmest, too.

The Caribbean Sea gets warmer and warmer as the sun passes over it on its way north in the spring-time. It is warmest during June and July. Then it cools slightly during the sun's summer stay up north. It warms up again during September and October as the sun passes over it once more on its way south. Then it cools again during the winter, when the sun is south of the equator. The times when it is warmest are the times when most of its hurricanes are born. That's why Caribbean hurricanes usually come during June and July, and again in September, October and November.

The ocean birthplace of the Cape Verde hurricanes is also warmed up twice each year — once as the sun moves over it on its way north, and again when the sun returns on its trip south. But in between these times, it is also warmed by ocean currents that bring it warm water from other parts of the ocean. So it has only one warmest season, instead of two like the Caribbean Sea. This season is during August and September, and this is when most of the Cape Verde hurricanes are born.

Most hurricanes start when a sea is warmest. But because the sea near the equator, even after cooling, is still very warm, hurricanes can start at other times as well. Caribbean hurricanes got an early start in 1955 when Alice was born on January fourth.

BIG AND SMALL LITTERS

Sometimes we hear about a lot of hurricanes in one year. Sometimes we hear about none at all. This is partly because the number of hurricanes that reach the coast changes from year to year. But it is also because the number of hurricanes born each year varies. In the Atlantic Ocean, the Gulf of Mexico and the Caribbean Sea together, there have been as few as two hurricanes in one year, and as many as twenty-one. There were only two in 1911, 1914, 1917, 1929 and 1930. There were twenty-one hurricanes in this area in 1933.

LIFE SPAN OF A HURRICANE

Hurricanes don't all last the same length of time. August hurricanes are usually the longest, with an average life of twelve days. July and November hurricanes last about eight days. The average life span for all hurricanes of the North Atlantic is nine and one-half days.

While the winds in a hurricane are very fast, the storm itself travels very slowly, usually from five to fifteen miles an hour. At fifteen miles an hour it can travel three hundred and sixty miles a day, and three thousand six hundred miles in ten days. The storm itself is usually more than three hundred miles wide. So, while hurricanes have a short life, they cover a lot of territory. We are lucky that they don't travel overland more often than they do.

WHY HURRICANES GO NORTH

Atlantic hurricanes start near the equator, but they don't stay there. They always go north. This happens because the air over the North Atlantic Ocean is like a giant wheel turning slowly all the time in the same direction as the hands of a clock. Hurricanes are born near the rim of the wheel, so they travel with the rim in a big circle. From the Cape Verde Islands, the rim moves west, crossing the ocean to the Caribbean Sea. From the Caribbean Sea it heads north, moving along the east coast of the United States. Then it moves east again, back across the Atlantic Ocean.

SINKING AIR

The center of this wheel of air is near the Azores Islands, west of Portugal. Here air from high up in

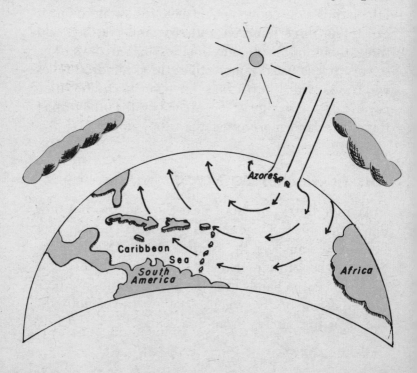

the atmosphere is always sinking. As it sinks, it piles up over the ocean, compressing the air that is there. The compressed air pushes out from this center and moves away in all directions. While the air is moving in this way, the rotation of the earth makes it turn like a wheel.

WHY HURRICANES RETURN TO THE OCEAN

We can understand why the wheel turns, by finding out why hurricanes that head north must always veer toward the east. If we look down on the earth from above the North Pole, the earth looks like a turning phonograph record, turning from west to east. The North Pole is the center of the record. A place near the North Pole travels around the center in a small circle. A place near the equator travels around the center in a large circle. Both places make a full circle in a day. Because the place near the equator travels a greater distance in a day, it is moving faster than the place near the pole. When a hurricane is near the equator, it moves eastward with the turning earth at this higher speed. When the hurricane moves north, it still turns around the pole at the same speed. But the ground that it is over then is nearer to the pole, and moves east more slowly. So the hurricane gets ahead of the ground. That's why it veers to the east and turns back to the Atlantic Ocean as it goes north.

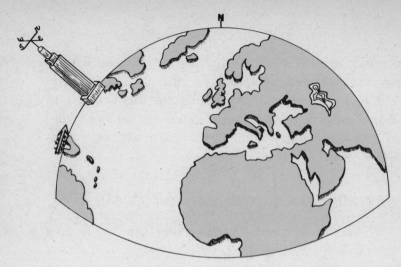

a) Hurricane heads north from Puerto Rico . . .

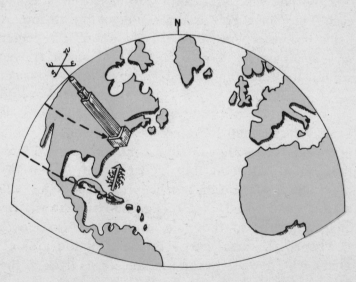

b) . . . and, as the earth turns, moves east as fast as Puerto Rico . . .

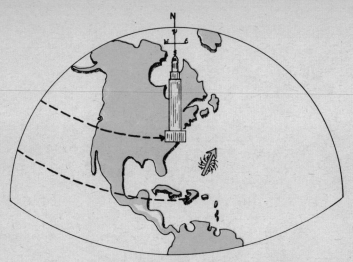

c)...New York, farther from the equator, moves east more
slowly than Puerto Rico...

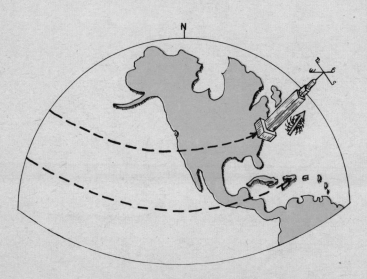

d) ...so Hurricane gets ahead of New York

57

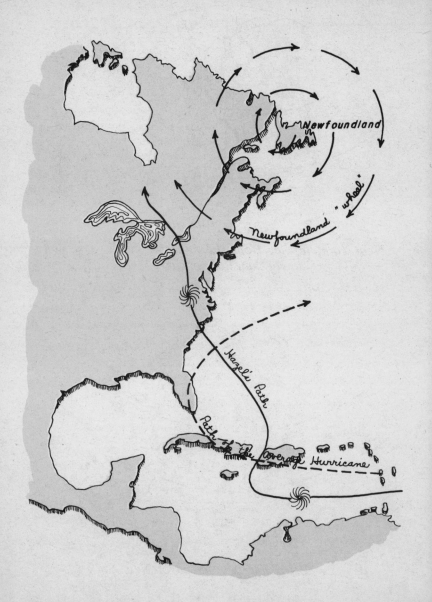

Newfoundland

Newfoundland "wheel"

Hazel's Path

Path of the average Hurricane

WHY HAZEL MISBEHAVED

Because of this veering to the east, very few hurricanes in the past were able to reach the New England states. By the time they got that far north, they were already back over the Atlantic Ocean. But in 1954, the hurricanes broke all the rules. One after the other, Carol, Edna and Hazel clung to the coast of the United States and stubbornly refused to turn east. Later the weathermen found out why. They discovered that currents in the upper air were piling up air near Newfoundland. This started another wheel of air turning, with Newfoundland as its center. The diagram shows how this wheel stopped the hurricanes from turning east and forced them to go farther north. It also made them move faster. Carol began as a slow-moving hurricane, traveling only three hundred miles in three days. Then, suddenly, she raced up the coast, covering four hundred miles in twelve hours.

5. PICTURE
OF A HURRICANE

RINGS WITHIN RINGS

THE drawing on page 62 shows what a hurricane looks like on a weather map. The lines you see on the map are called *isobars*. All the places on one line have the same air pressure at the ground. Places on different lines have different air pressures. The hurricane is marked by the group of small circles one within the other. The pressure at each circle is higher than along a circle inside it. It is lower than along a circle that surrounds it. The air pressure is lowest in the center of the smallest circle. This place is called the "eye" of the hurricane. On the map it looks like the bull's-eye on a target.

WHAT MAKES AIR PRESSURE

To understand what happens in a hurricane we have to understand about air pressure. Air pressure is the result of two things, the weight of the air and the "spring" of the air.

Air has weight. Where you have a big pile of air, it presses down with all its weight on whatever it rests on. The air above the ground is really quite a big pile. It reaches up in the sky for over two hundred miles. To measure how hard the air presses down, weathermen use an instrument called a *barometer*. A barometer may be made out of a dish, a glass tube about a yard long, closed at one end, and the heavy liquid metal mercury. First the dish and the glass tube are filled with mercury. Then the tube is placed in an upright position, with its open end in the dish, under the surface of the mercury. The mercury in the tube doesn't all run into the dish. The pressure of the air on the mercury in the dish is strong enough to hold up a column of mercury in the tube. In fact, the stronger the pressure, the higher the column of mercury it can hold up. So weathermen measure air pressure by measuring the number of inches in the column of mercury. At sea level it is usually about thirty inches high. Weighing this amount of mercury shows that the air presses down on each square inch with a force of about fifteen pounds. The pressure of the air is always changing. The weathermen measure

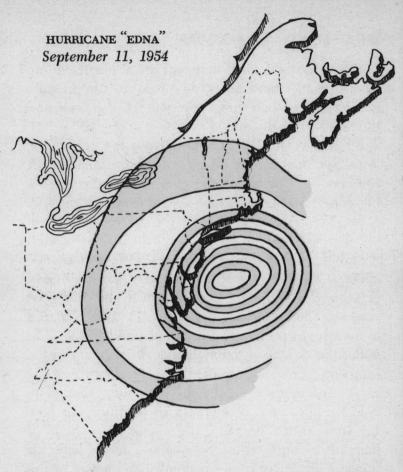

HURRICANE "EDNA"
September 11, 1954

the changes and announce them in their weather reports. When a weather report says that the barometric pressure is 29.75, it means that the air presses down hard enough to hold up a column of mercury 29.75 inches high. When the barometer is "rising" it means that the air is pressing down harder and harder as time passes. When the barometer is "falling" the air presses down with less and less force.

The air is also like a coiled spring. If you have air in a container, you can squeeze it, or compress it, the way you can compress a coiled spring. Like a coiled spring, too, the air pushes back as you press on it, until the push back balances the force with which you press on it. Air that is near the ground is being squeezed or compressed by the weight of all the air that is on top of it. It pushes back hard enough to balance this weight and hold it up. So "air pressure" has a double meaning. It means the weight of the air pressing down on a square inch of ground. It also means the push back by the "spring" of the air.

WHY AIR IS LIKE A SPRING

Air is like a spring because it is made up of tiny pieces, called *molecules,* separated by big spaces and moving rapidly in all directions all the time. When air is in a container, the moving molecules keep bumping against the sides of the container. This constant bumping is the outward push you feel when you try to squeeze the air into a smaller space. It is the "spring" of the air that gives it its pressure. When you squeeze a lot of air into a small space, the molecules become more crowded. Then they bombard the sides of the container more often, so the pressure increases. This is what happens when you pump up the tires of a bicycle or a car. If you press your finger against a tire as you pump it, you can feel how the air pushes out harder and harder as you force more air in. When you spread out air in a larger space, the molecules become less crowded. Then they bombard the sides of the container less often, so the pressure falls.

WHAT HAPPENS AT THE "EYE"

The "eye" of a hurricane is the center of the storm. It is like a big, invisible pipe, about ten miles high and about fourteen miles wide. Air at the bottom is rising into the pipe. Air at the top is sinking into the pipe. The two currents of air, one rising, the other sinking, meet about five miles above the ground and flow out at that level away from the eye. At the ground the upward movement of the air keeps it from pressing down with its full weight. That's why the air pressure is low in the eye of the hurricane. It may be as low as twenty-eight inches.

A TUG OF WAR IN THE AIR

In a tug of war, two teams pull on a rope in opposite directions. If one team pulls harder than the other, the rope begins to move toward that team.

You can have another kind of tug of war by using a pole instead of a rope, and by pushing instead of pulling. Then, if one team pushes harder than the other, the pole will move toward the team with the weaker push. There is a tug of war like this in the air surrounding a hurricane. The "pole" is the air along any straight line from the eye of the hurricane to a place outside the hurricane. The "teams" consist of the air at both ends of the line. Because air pressure pushes out in all directions, each "team" is pushing against the line of air between them. The air at the eye is pushing against this line of air, trying to push it away from the eye. The air outside the storm is trying to push it toward the eye. But the air pressure at the eye is lower than the air pressure outside the storm, so the push from the eye is weaker. The stronger push from the outside makes the whole line of air move toward the eye. This is why there are winds rushing toward the eye of a hurricane.

SPINNING LIKE A TOP

If the earth were standing still, the winds of a hurricane would blow toward the eye along straight lines coming together like spokes of a wheel, as in diagram A on the next page. But the earth doesn't stand still. It rotates on its axis. The rotation of the earth turns the ground under the winds, so it makes the winds veer. North of the equator, a wind headed north veers to the east, in the same way that a hurricane moving north veers to the east. A wind headed south veers to the west. This is shown in diagram B. So the winds don't flow directly to the eye, but spiral around it, turning the hurricane into a giant whirlwind, as shown in diagram C. This makes the whole mass of air in the storm spin like a top. In the northern hemisphere, this spinning is opposite to the direction in which the hands of a clock move, so it is called counterclockwise. In the southern hemisphere the rotation of the earth has an opposite effect. So a hurricane in the southern hemisphere spins in the same direction as the hands of a clock, or clockwise.

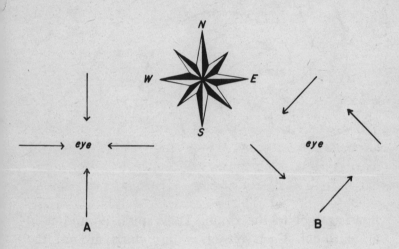

AN UPSIDE-DOWN DRAIN

You can get a good picture of a hurricane in action in your bathroom sink. Fill the sink with water, and then open the drain. As the water flows down the drain, streams of water flow toward the drain from all parts of the basin. But they don't

C. *The Winds of a Hurricane*

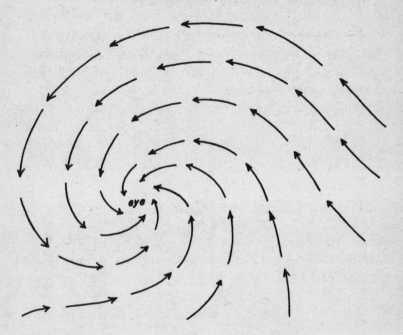

flow straight to the drain. They spiral around it in a whirlpool. Each bit of water whirls around the drain and gets closer and closer until it is sucked down into the drain. Now imagine the sink turned upside down, and you have a picture of a hurricane. In a hurricane the eye is like the drain of the sink, but air flows *up* from the ground into the eye. The surrounding air spirals around it in a whirlwind. Each bit of air whirls around the eye and gets closer and closer until it is sucked up into the eye.

A HURRICANE SITS FOR A PORTRAIT

We can show a hurricane on a map. The lines on the map, showing places that have the same pressure, make it look like a bull's-eye. We can make drawings showing how the winds of a hurricane move. These drawings make the hurricane look like a whirlpool. To find out what a hurricane really looks like from far off we would have to take a photograph of one. This has actually been done by radar. The photographic image of a hurricane on a radar screen is shown in the pictorial section following page 35. It shows the arrangement of the clouds in the storm. Since the clouds ride on the backs of the winds, the picture shows clearly the spiral paths the winds take around the eye.

6. A GIANT HEAT ENGINE

A LOT of work is done for us today by steam engines, gasoline engines and Diesel engines. These are all *heat engines* that turn heat into motion. A hurricane is also a heat engine, because it turns the heat of the sun into the motion of the winds.

NATURE'S HOT-WATER BOTTLE

When you go to bed in the wintertime, if your feet are cold, you may put a hot-water bottle next to them. Then the heat in the hot water will flow into your feet and make them warm. The hot-water bottle is useful because it passes some of its heat on to anything cooler that presses against it. Down near the equator, the sea acts like a big hot-water bottle. It passes some of its heat on to the air that presses against it.

The heat of the sea comes originally from the sun. Rays of heat and light leave the sun and travel ninety-three million miles through empty space to get to the earth. When they reach the earth, they pass first through the air, and then they fall on the sea or on the land. Air is not a good heat-catcher, so it catches very little of this heat, and allows a lot of it to pass right through. Water is a better heat-catcher, so the rays that fall on the sea are caught, and the heat is stored in the water. As more and more heat is caught, the water becomes warmer and warmer. At night, when no more sunlight is caught, the water cools off a little. But the next day, when the sun is up again, the water is warmed again, and it makes up for the loss of heat at night.

The air above the sea stands on top of the water and reaches up for miles into the sky. The lower level, or foot, of the air is pressed against the surface of the water. Some of the heat of the water flows into the lower level of the air and makes it warm. Near the equator, where the sea is warmer than in any other part of the world, the air above the sea becomes warmer, too.

THE HOT AIR BEGINS TO RISE

The air is made up of molecules that are moving around in all directions all the time. When the air is made warmer, the molecules move faster. When they move faster, they press harder against anything that the air touches. This makes the pressure in the lower level of the air higher. Before the air became warmer, the pressure in the lower level of the air was just enough to hold up the weight of the air pressing down on it. Now the pressure in the lower level pushes up harder than the weight above it pushes down. It pushes the air on top of it out of the way, and makes room for itself to spread out or expand. When it expands, the same amount of air is spread out in a larger space. Because the molecules in this space are less crowded, the pressure falls, until it again just balances the weight of the air on top. But now, because the air is spread out in a larger space, each part of this space has less air in it than it had before. So the spread-out air is lighter than the more closely packed air that surrounds it. The heavier air pushes in under the lighter air and makes it rise off the ground. That's why, when the air near the sea becomes warm, it becomes lighter and begins to rise.

A ONE-EYED GIANT IS BORN

Where the air rises, it lifts some of the weight of the air off the ground. Then the air there doesn't press down as hard as it did before, and the pressure at the ground falls. Where the pressure is low, the air loses the tug of war. The surrounding air, which has a higher pressure, pushes air toward the place where the pressure is low. So winds begin to blow, bringing air in to take the place of the air that is rising off the ground. The center of the rising stream of air becomes the eye of the hurricane. About five miles above the ground, the rising air meets a stream of air coming down from higher levels. Both streams of air then flow out away from the eye, making room for more of the rising air. The winds on the ground that rush toward the eye veer because of the rotation of the earth. As they spiral around the eye, the whole mass of air, for hundreds of miles around, spins like a top. Meanwhile, this spinning top is embedded in the big wheel of air that covers the North Atlantic Ocean. As the wheel slowly turns, it carries the spinning hurricane around in a big circle.

Two thousand years ago the people who lived in Greece used to tell stories about the Cyclops. The Cyclops were supposed to be one-eyed giants who helped the god of fire make thunderbolts in his workshop. These giants were not real. They were products of the imagination of the Greek storytellers. Hurricanes are real one-eyed giants. They are not alive, but they are bigger, more powerful and more terrible than the Greeks ever dreamed a giant could be. And hurricanes make their own thunderbolts, too, in the thunderstorms that rage in them.

THE HURRICANE WITH TWO EYES

Hazel and most of her sister hurricanes of 1954 were ordinary one-eyed giants. But Edna was different. Edna started her career with one eye, and followed in Carol's footsteps along the east coast of the United States. But when she reached the New England states she suddenly became twins. Her eye split and formed two separate eyes. Then, while winds spiraled in toward each eye, the two eyes slowly turned around each other. The people in New England were not pleased to get two hurricanes for the price of one.

FINDING THE EYE

When a hurricane comes close to where you live, you may want to know where the center of the storm is. Of course you can find out by listening to a weather report over the radio. But you can also find out by yourself, by noticing the direction of the wind where you are.

Some people think the center of the storm would be found where the wind is coming from. This isn't true at all. If you look at the wind diagram on page 68, you will see that the winds go toward the center of the storm, not away from it. And even then, because of the rotation of the earth, they don't go directly toward it, but spiral around it. In the northern hemisphere, to find the direction of the eye of the hurricane, *stand with your back to the wind. Then the eye of the storm will be on your left.*

THE HORN CARD

Because a hurricane is a whirlwind, the winds in different parts of the storm have different speeds and different directions. The wind diagram on page 68 shows that winds on opposite sides of the eye blow in opposite directions. The winds nearest the eye are the strongest. So, when a hurricane passes by, the winds keep changing in direction and speed.

When a ship is caught in a hurricane, it is important for the sailors to know what kind of winds to expect. They can figure out how the wind will change by using a "horn card" somewhat like the one on page 76. The horn card is really a map of a typical hurricane, printed on something transparent like celluloid. The arrows on the horn card show the direction of the wind in each part of the hurricane. The number of feathers on each arrow show the speed of the wind, following the code explained on page 117. The sailor who uses the horn card first finds

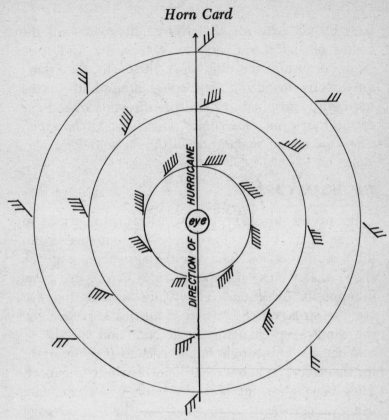

out from a weather report where the center of the hurricane is, and which way it is moving. Next he puts the horn card on a map at the place where the hurricane is. Then he moves the card in the direction in which the storm is moving. As he moves the card he can see what the wind will be like at any place that the storm will pass over.

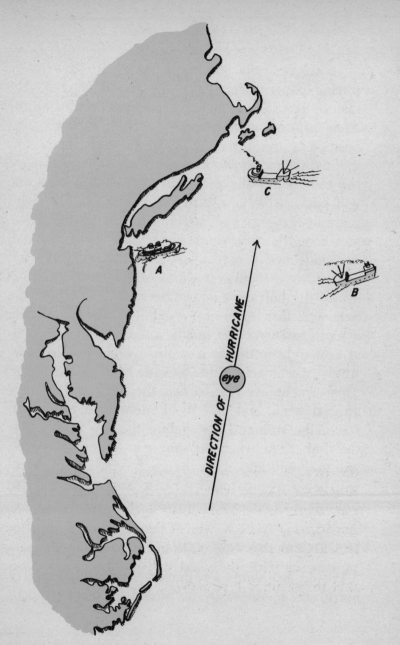

To see how the horn card works, first trace it on tracing paper. Then place the traced copy on the map on page 77, so that the center circle rests on the circle printed on the map. This will show the first position of the hurricane. Then move the horn card in the direction shown by the big arrow. As you move the card you will see that the eye of the hurricane will pass east of the position of ship A. The wind there at first will be a north wind. As the hurricane moves north, the wind at A will swing around, becoming first a northwest wind, then a west wind and finally a southwest wind. At the same time, the eye of the hurricane is passing west of B. There the wind will first be an east wind. Then it will become a southeast wind and finally a south wind. The ship at C is right in the path of the eye of the hurricane. At first it will have winds blowing from the northeast. Then, as the eye approaches, the wind will become an east wind, and will blow stronger and stronger. It will be strongest just before the eye passes over the ship. Then, when the ship is in the eye, the wind will suddenly stop. After the eye has passed, the wind will begin again from the west, and then will lose force as it becomes a southwest wind.

THE STORM DID NOT COME BACK

People who are not familiar with the ways of hurricanes might easily be misled by what happens at ship C. A landlubber on ship C would notice that at the height of the storm the wind is blowing from the east. Thinking that the storm moves in the direction of the wind, he would believe that the storm is coming from the east. When the wind stops, he would think that the storm has already passed. Then, when the wind starts blowing from the west, he

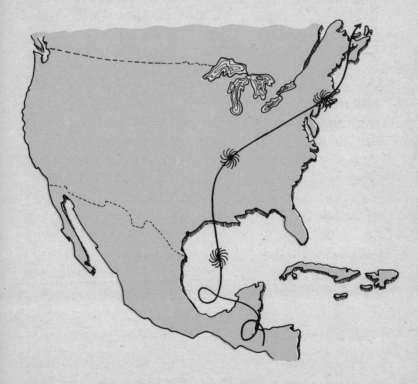

Loop Hurricane, June 4-21, 1934

would think that the storm has "come back." Actually, the storm is not moving east or west, but is moving north. And when the landlubber thinks that the storm has passed, the ship is actually in the center of the storm.

Although this storm did not "come back," there are records of storms that did. The loop hurricane described on page 34 passed over Cuba, then made a loop, and came back to pass over Cuba again. Another hurricane, in June, 1934, actually made two loops, as it traveled from Central America across the Gulf of Mexico into the United States.

ALL CLEAR........

STORM HEADS OUT TO SEA

WIND-DRIVEN SPEAR: Hurricane winds in Puerto Rico drove a pine board ten feet long, three inches wide, and one inch thick right through the trunk of this palm tree. (September 13, 1928.)

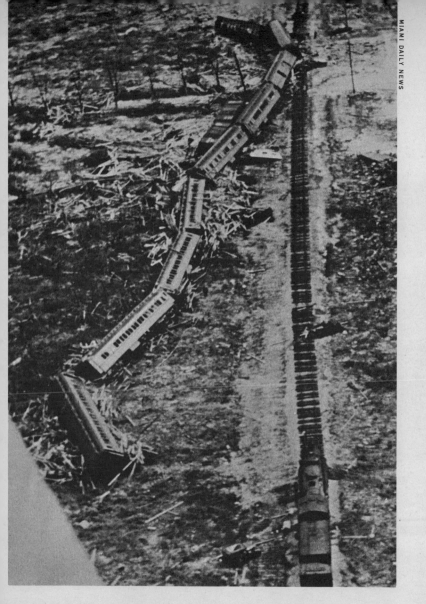

RESCUE TRAIN WRECKED: On its way to the Florida Keys to rescue hundreds of people trapped by a hurricane, this train was swept off the tracks by storm winds. (September 2, 1935.)

UNDER WATER: This is the parking field at La Guardia Airport in New York after a hurricane. Sometimes as much rain will fall in a hurricane in one day as some cities get in a whole year. (September 1, 1954.)

HIGH AND DRY: These fishing vessels in Massachusetts were hurled ashore by Carol's fury. When the storm waves swept over the land they carried the ships with them, leaving them stranded on shore.

AFTER THE STORM: In the unpredictable path of a storm, one house is lifted right off its foundation while the house next door is unharmed. (August 29, 1955.)

WIND BITES METAL: A violent wind twisted the Tacoma Narrows Bridge into weird shapes before the bridge collapsed on November 7, 1940.

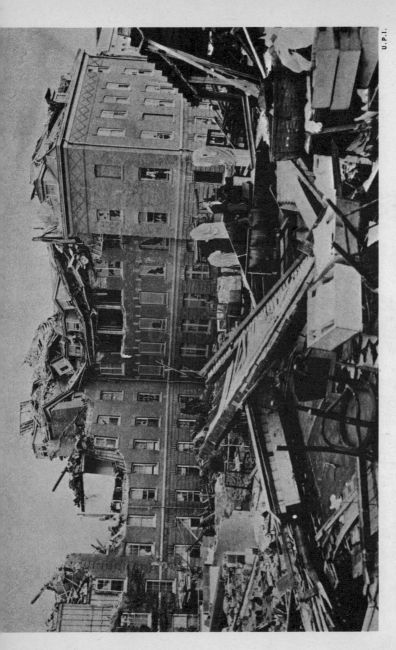

A TORNADO STRIKES: This solid brick building at Worcester, Massachusetts, caved in under the blows of a tornado. (June 11, 1953.)

7. HOW A HURRICANE FEEDS ITSELF

INVISIBLE WATER

WHEN you wipe the top of your kitchen table with a damp cloth, you spread a thin film of water over it. Then, as you watch it, you can see the film of water shrink and finally disappear. The water vanishes, as if by magic. What has happened is that, one by one, the molecules of water have jumped off the tabletop, and have scattered in the air. When the molecules were close together on the table, they formed liquid water which you could see. When the molecules scattered, they formed a gas called *water vapor* which you could not see. Because the liquid water has turned into vapor, we say it has *evaporated*.

The water at the surface of the sea evaporates, too. The air above it soaks it up like a sponge, and holds it in the form of water vapor. Warm air can hold more water than cool air. So, near the equator, where the air is warm, the air over the sea soaks up a lot of water, and becomes moist air.

WET AIR IS LIGHTER

Molecules of water weigh less than most of the molecules of gas that are found in the air. So, when air soaks up a lot of water vapor, it becomes lighter. In Chapter VI we saw how air that is warmed up becomes lighter and begins to rise. If the air soaks up water at the same time, it becomes lighter still, and rises even faster. When a hurricane is born, heat and water vapor work together to start the rising current of air that becomes the center of the storm.

FANNING THE SEA

Wet air is like a sponge filled with water. When it has all the water it can hold, it can't soak up any more. So, when the air over some water has soaked up as much as it has room for, the water stops evaporating. We can make more water evaporate by pushing the wet air away and moving dry air in to take its place. That's why we can make a wet tabletop dry faster by fanning it. The fanning starts a small wind that carries the wet air away and brings in fresh, dry air that will soak up more water. The winds of a hurricane fan the surface of the sea in the same way. They travel over hundreds of miles of water, picking up moisture as they go. Then, while the wet air rises near the eye of the hurricane, the fresh, dry air follows and picks up more moisture. As long as a hurricane remains at sea, its winds feed it a steady supply of water vapor.

SQUEEZING THE SPONGE

When a sponge is full of water, you can squeeze some water out by crushing the sponge in your hand. When you crush the sponge you make the spaces in it smaller, and then it can't hold as much water as it did before. Any amount of water above what it can hold drips out. When air is full of water, you can squeeze water out of it, too, by cooling the air. Cool air can't hold as much water vapor as warm air. So, as air is cooled, any amount of water vapor above what it can hold comes out of the air in little drops of liquid water. When this happens we say the water vapor has *condensed.*

Near the eye of a hurricane the moist, warm air is rising. But as it rises, it expands and cools. When it cools, some of its moisture is squeezed out of it. The water vapor that condenses forms tiny droplets that float in the air in great clouds.

HIDDEN HEAT

When you heat some water in a pot on a stove, as the heat flows into the water, at first the level of heat, the temperature of the water, rises. When the temperature reaches two hundred and twelve degrees Fahrenheit, the water begins to boil. Then, as you put more heat into the water, the temperature no longer rises. Instead, all the additional heat is used up in changing liquid water into water vapor. It is stored in the vapor that bubbles out of the pot. This stored-up heat that is hidden in the vapor is called the *latent heat of evaporation.*

You don't have to boil water to make it evaporate. All you have to do is let it stand in dry air. Then some of the water molecules jump into the air, and the air soaks them up. This is what happens when you wave a wet hand in the air until your hand is dry. But even then the water needs heat to make it evaporate. This time it gets the heat it needs by taking heat away from your hand. That's why a wet hand begins to feel cool.

The hidden heat remains in the water only as long as the water stays in vapor form. When the vapor condenses to liquid water again, it gives the heat back. So, as water condenses out of rising air, and forms clouds, the condensing water gives out heat. This heat of condensation makes the air warmer and gives it another upward push. But as long as the air keeps moving up, it lifts some of the weight of the air off the ground. This keeps the air pressure at the ground low, and the winds continue to blow in from places where the pressure is high. That's why a hurricane continues to grow as long as it remains over the sea. The winds that pass over the water bring it a steady supply of water vapor. The hidden heat in the water vapor builds up the power of the storm.

TOWERING CLOUDS

As the air rises in the center of a hurricane, the heat given out when water condenses pushes the air higher and higher. But as it climbs some more, it cools some more, and squeezes out more water. So clouds are formed at higher and higher levels. Great towering clouds are formed that reach up about forty thousand feet above the ground. At the highest levels, the air is so cold that when the water condenses it becomes ice. So the highest clouds are made up of ice crystals instead of droplets of water.

ICE CRYSTALS START THE RAIN

The water droplets formed in a cloud are very small and light, and float easily on the air. They are not heavy enough to push their way through the air to reach the ground. So, as long as there are only water droplets in the clouds, no rain will fall. But when the rising air climbs high enough to form ice crystals, then rain begins to fall. The ice crystals pull many water droplets onto themselves, and form big drops of water. The big drops are too heavy to be held back by the resistance of the air, and their weight pulls them down to the ground. So, out of the towering clouds in a hurricane, torrents of rain pour down in a steady stream.

SPINNING AWAY FROM THE EYE

The air that flows along the ground into the eye of a hurricane is carried in by the whirling winds. As it rises in the eye it continues to whirl around and around. When it reaches a height of about twenty-five thousand feet it begins to move away from the eye, and makes room for more air that is whirling up behind it.

To understand why the whirling air leaves the eye when it gets high up, try this simple experiment. Cut the bottom off a round cardboard cereal box to make a wide cylinder open at both ends. Hold the cylinder against a small, flat board, and place a marble inside. By swinging the cyclinder, pressed against the board, around in circles, you can make the marble whirl around inside. Now place the cylinder and board on a flat table. The marble will continue to whirl around, rolling against the inside of the cylinder.

Then, if you suddenly lift the cylinder away from the board, the marble will shoot off away from the center around which it has been whirling. The whirling marble was always trying to get away from the center, but the cylinder was holding it back. When the cylinder stopped holding it back, the marble was free to shoot off. The whirling air rising in the eye of a hurricane is like the whirling marble. It, too, is trying to get away from the center. But near the ground, the air pressure in the eye is lower than the pressure outside the storm. The air pushed in from all sides by the high pressure outside is like the cardboard cylinder. It keeps the whirling air in the eye from pushing out. But high up above the ground, the pressure in the eye is not much different from the pressure outside at that level. The whirling air is not held back. It's as though the cylinder were removed, and the whirling air flows away from the eye.

THE HURRICANE'S VEIL

As the air flows away from the eye high above the ground, it still rises slowly. Water vapor continues to condense out of it, and forms a thin sheet of cloud made up of ice crystals. The farther away the air flows, the higher and thinner the cloud becomes. Several hundred miles away from the eye, the cloud is just a thin veil surrounding the storm, and it is

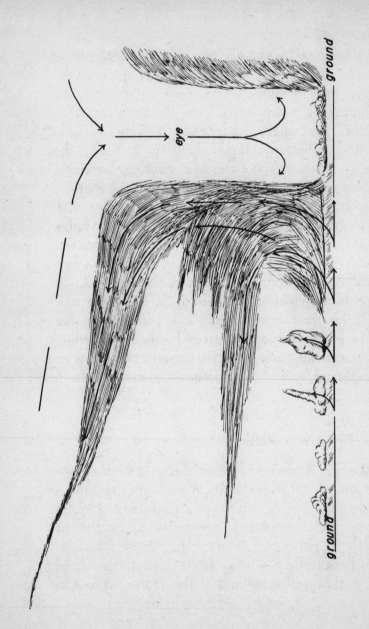

The Clouds of a Hurricane

about fifty thousand feet above the ground. When a hurricane approaches, this high veil of ice crystals is the first part of it that you can see.

A HURRICANE DESTROYS ITSELF

When a hurricane invades the coast, it destroys not only people and property. It also destroys itself. As long as it remains over the sea, its winds keep feeding it water vapor. The heat given out when the vapor condenses keeps the storm alive and builds up its great power. But when the storm moves in over the land, it loses its supply of water vapor. Without a steady supply of the heat that is hidden in the vapor, the hurricane begins to die. But it doesn't die peacefully. Unfortunately it kills many people before it becomes weak enough to be harmless.

8. HURRICANE HUNTERS

FEELING THE PULSE OF THE AIR

WHEN a doctor examines a patient who is sick, he looks for clues that will help him figure out what is happening in the patient's body. He takes the patient's pulse, measures his temperature and looks at his throat. There are many other ways, too, in which he gathers facts about the condition of the patient's body. All these facts that he collects are like the parts of a jigsaw puzzle. When he puts them together he gets a picture of what is happening. When he understands what is happening, he knows how to protect the patient against his disease.

A hurricane is like a sickness of the air. To protect ourselves against the damage it can do, we try to understand how it develops and grows, and how and why it moves. So we have doctors of the air, called *meteorologists,* who work for the Weather Bureau. They look for clues in the air the way a doctor looks for clues in the body. They set up weather stations in many places on shore. At these stations they take measurements to see what the pressure of the air is, how warm it is and how much water vapor is in it. They also measure the strength and direction of the wind, and see what kind of clouds are in the sky. When they put all these facts together, they have a picture of what is happening in the air.

WEATHER EYES AT SEA

There are weather stations at sea, too. Every ship is a weather station. It carries the instruments needed to measure the state of the air, and it sends out radio messages to report the facts it gathers. In this way the Weather Bureau keeps track of what is happening in the air over the sea. This is important for the study of hurricanes, because all hurricanes begin over the sea.

WEATHER STATIONS IN THE SKY

A hurricane isn't only on the ground. It extends up into the air for miles. What happens high up in the air has a great influence on what happens down near the ground. So it is important to find out what is going on in the upper levels of the air, too. To get this information, the Weather Bureau, working with the U.S. Navy and the U.S. Air Force, sends weather stations up into the air. One way of doing this is to send up a small weather station without men. It is called a *radiosonde*, and consists of measuring instruments and a radio transmitter, all carried by a balloon. As the balloon rises in the air, the transmitter automatically reports the measurements being taken by the instruments. Another way is to send up a weather station with men, in an airplane. The plane flies into the storm area to make observations at different heights. The men in the plane can also observe what is happening far away by means of radar. They send out radio waves which travel out ahead of them. When the waves strike a cloud, they bounce back. The radar receiver in the plane picks up the waves that bounce back and uses them to form a picture on the radar screen. In this way the men can actually see the arrangement of the clouds in a hurricane many miles away.

IN A HURRICANE'S EYE

To understand a hurricane, you have to understand what is happening in its eye. So, lately, weather men have purposely gone into the eye of a hurricane to see what is going on there. This was first done in 1944, when a radiosonde was released in the eye of a hurricane at Tampa, Florida. The balloon rose fifty-six thousand feet and sent out a steady stream of radio messages about the temperature, pressure and moisture it found at different levels.

In 1947, the Air Weather Service sent a plane into the eye of an Atlantic hurricane. The plane made several trips into the eye, cruising about at different levels. In 1951, a plane flew into the eye of the Pacific typhoon, Marge, and stayed in the eye for four and a half hours.

The typhoon, Marge, was the third largest typhoon in Weather Bureau records. The eye in this typhoon was forty miles wide. The plane entered the eye at an altitude of eleven thousand feet. In the eye itself, the sky above the plane was clear, but it was surrounded by a circular wall of clouds rising thirty-five thousand feet into the air. Below the plane, a layer of low clouds partly hid the surface of the ocean. Where the water could be seen through breaks in the clouds, it was tossing about violently. The air in the eye was very much warmer than the surrounding air. At eight thousand feet above sea level it was warmer by fourteen degrees Fahrenheit. At eighteen thousand feet it was thirty-two degrees warmer. A radar picture of the clouds in the hurricane showed clearly how the winds spiral around and into the eye.

To find clues about the way in which a hurricane moves, the explorers studied the air outside Marge's eye, too. They found an important clue five hundred miles away from the eye. There, at an altitude of fifty thousand feet, and ahead of Marge in the direction in which she was moving, was a low-pressure area. This upper-air low-pressure area seemed to be steering the hurricane as it traveled over the ground.

The facts the weather men have found so far are like a jigsaw puzzle that has many pieces missing. They form only an incomplete picture of how hurricanes grow and move. Weather men hope to find more of the missing facts by taking more measurements in the eyes of hurricanes and in the upper air that surrounds them.

EYES OPEN FOR TROUBLE

To be able to warn people in time if a hurricane is heading their way, the Weather Bureau keeps a close watch on the places where hurricanes usually begin. A special hurricane-forecasting unit works in Miami, Florida, with the help of the U.S. Navy and the U.S. Air Force. It collects information about the weather in the Caribbean Sea and the Atlantic Ocean. At the first sign that a hurricane is born, airplanes are sent out to bring back more information.

If a hurricane starts moving north, the Miami station sends out the first hurricane warnings. When the storm passes Cape Hatteras, North Carolina, the

U.S. Weather Bureau station at Washington National Airport takes over responsibility. After the storm passes Block Island, Rhode Island, the warnings are issued by the Weather Bureau Airport Station in Boston, Massachusetts.

RIDING THE BACK OF A HURRICANE

When a hurricane threatens the coast, hurricane hunters in Air Force and Navy planes take off from bases such as Jacksonville, Florida, and Bermuda to fly into the storm. They fly through the eye twice a day, and stay with the storm, getting up-to-the-minute information about its movements, until it strikes the coast. Sometimes they release balloons carrying radar reflectors to make it easier to see the storm on a radar screen.

SIGNS OF AN APPROACHING HURRICANE

The people who live on the coast of the Gulf of Mexico have had more experience with hurricanes than they care for. As a result of this experience, they have learned to recognize certain signs that a hurricane is on its way. Some of these signs are in the water, others are in the sky.

One sign is in the tides. If the tide rises higher than usual, it may mean that there is a hurricane nearby. Another sign is in the waves that break on the shore. In the Gulf of Mexico, waves usually roll up the beach with a steady rhythm of twelve to fifteen waves a minute. If the rhythm slows down, and only four or five long swells come in each minute, then it means there is a hurricane somewhere behind the swells.

In the air, the first sign of an approaching hurricane is the high veil of ice-crystal clouds that moves out ahead of the storm. When the storm comes closer, a bar of low clouds appears on the horizon. Later, there are gusty winds and showers. When the hurricane is close, the air pressure falls and strong winds begin to blow.

When any of these signs appear, it is time to listen to the weather report. If the Weather Bureau warns that a hurricane is moving inland, we can't stop the storm from coming, but we can try to protect ourselves from its fury. We can't keep a storm wave from flooding the shore, but, if we are warned early enough, we can get out of reach of the water. We can't stop the wind from blowing down trees, but we can try to avoid being under them when they fall. We can't prevent the wind from tearing down power lines, but we can keep away from live wires that lie on the ground. We can't stop a hurricane from doing great damage, but by being careful we can reduce the amount of damage that it does.

9. THE TORNADO:

MIGHTY MIDGET

IT is a curious fact that the storms that do the most damage are either the biggest or the smallest members of the storm family. The biggest storms are the hurricanes. They are giants that are hundreds of miles wide and travel thousands of miles. The smallest are the tornadoes. They are midgets, usually no more than twelve hundred feet wide, and they generally travel only about sixteen miles before they die. But, small as they are, they are very powerful and often kill more people and destroy more property than many hurricanes do.

The worst tornadoes the United States ever had occurred on March 18, 1925. Three of them struck, one after the other, along a path two hundred and nineteen miles long through Missouri, Illinois and Indiana. They killed six hundred and eighty-nine people, injured two thousand people, and destroyed property worth sixteen and one-half million dollars.

A GIANT VACUUM CLEANER

A tornado begins with a funnel-shaped cloud that forms high up in the air and then roars down to the ground. In the center of the funnel, air is moving up at high speed, sometimes as fast as five hundred miles an hour. The suction of this upward-rushing air makes the tornado act like a giant vacuum cleaner. It can pick up a house or a truck as easily as an ordinary vacuum cleaner picks up pieces of paper or dust. Because it sucks up large amounts of dust from the ground it crosses, the funnel of a tornado is dark and can be seen miles away.

While the air in the funnel rushes up from the ground, the surrounding air near the ground flows in to take its place. The winds blow in toward the funnel of a tornado the way winds blow in toward the eye of a hurricane. Because of the rotation of the earth, they spiral into the funnel. So a tornado, like a hurricane, is a whirlwind. That's why it is often called a *twister*.

HOUSES THAT EXPLODE

When a tornado destroys a house, it doesn't blow it down the way a hurricane does. It makes the house *explode.* The air that surrounds a house usually presses against it with a force of about fifteen pounds on every square inch. At the same time the air inside the house presses out just as hard. As long as the air is undisturbed, the pressure from the inside is balanced by the pressure from the outside. But when a tornado passes over a house, the air that surrounds the house is suddenly sucked away. The pressure of the air inside the house still pushes out against the walls, but there is not as much pressure pushing back from the outside. The walls are then pushed out in an explosion. When a hurricane destroys a house, the house is wrecked, but it still looks like a house. When a tornado destroys a house, there is no house left to be seen. The explosion blows it to bits. Many of the pieces of the house are sucked up into the funnel of the tornado and carried away. The rest of the pieces lie scattered on the ground. Often only a bare foundation is left where the house once stood.

TORNADO PRANKS

The high winds of a tornado give it the power to do many strange things. One tornado lifted a cow off the ground, carried it across a field and then let it down at the other end of the field. The tornado of June 8, 1953, which struck the states of Michigan and Ohio, hurled a car through the woods and blew heavy trucks off the road. It carried one heavy truck, loaded with freight, a distance of four hundred feet. When the truck was found, there was no trace of the driver.

In the same way that a hurricane wind can turn a piece of wood into a spear, a tornado wind can turn a straw into a bullet. *Tornadoes have been known to drive straws right through thick wooden boards.*

TWISTERS IN A HURRICANE

It is bad enough when a town is hit by a hurricane. It is just as bad to be hit by a tornado. But imagine what it is like to be struck by a hurricane and a tornado at the same time! This can actually happen, because sometimes there are tornadoes within a hurricane. On September 10, 1919, a tornado developed in a hurricane at Goulds, Florida, twenty miles southwest of Miami. The tornado tore sheet-metal roofs off the houses and wrapped them around trees a mile away.

TWISTERS AT SEA

Sometimes tornadoes are formed at sea. A funnel-shaped cloud descends from the sky until it reaches the surface of the water. There the suction of the air rising in the funnel pulls water up from the surface of the sea. The narrow, whirling cloud that looks like a pipe joining the sky to the sea is called a *waterspout*. When the master of a ship sights a waterspout, he tries to keep as far away from it as possible.

WHERE TORNADOES COME FROM

Most of the tornadoes in the United States occur in the central and southeastern states. During the period from 1916 to 1950, Kansas had one hundred and sixty tornadoes, the highest number of any state. Iowa was second with one hundred and thirty-five tornadoes. Other states that have had many tornadoes are Nebraska, Oklahoma, Missouri, South Dakota and Minnesota.

This region is a battleground between two different kinds of air. Warm, moist air comes in from the Gulf of Mexico and the Caribbean Sea. Cold, dry air comes south from Canada. They meet over the land and push against each other. Sometimes the cold air pushes the warm air out of the way. At other times the warm air makes the cold air retreat back north. Most of the changes in weather in the United States arise from this constant battle of warm air versus cold air. Tornadoes are also a product of this battle.

HOW TORNADOES ARE BORN

Cold air is heavier than warm air. So, when cold air comes up against warm air, it usually pushes its

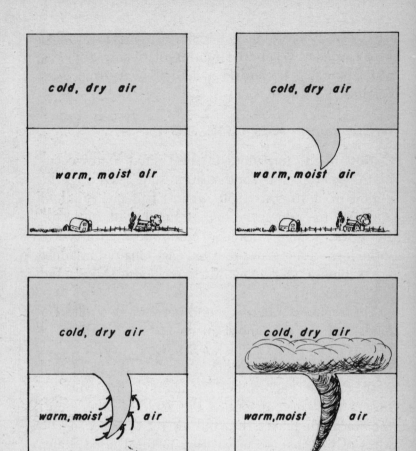

BIRTH OF A TORNADO

way under the warm air. But sometimes the opposite happens, and the cold air rolls *over* the warm air about a mile above the ground. When this happens, there is always the danger that tornadoes may develop. If a tongue of the cold air breaks through into the warm air, the lighter warm air surrounding the tongue will begin to float up into the tongue. As the warm air rises in the tongue it becomes cooler, and the water vapor in it is squeezed out. Droplets of water form to make a cloud. When the cloud develops, the tongue of air can be seen as the funnel-shaped cloud that marks the beginning of a tornado. As the warm air next to the funnel is drawn into it, the air right under it moves up to take its place. In this way the suction of the funnel reaches lower and lower levels, and the funnel is seen to drop down to the ground. The whirling, rising air in the funnel becomes dark with the dust it picks up as it smashes houses and uproots trees. Once it is formed, the funnel moves along the ground, usually from southwest to northeast, at a speed between twenty-five and forty miles an hour.

RAIN, THUNDER AND LIGHTNING

Water vapor is squeezed out of the rising air in the tornado cloud. But when vapor condenses to form drops of water, it gives out heat. The heat makes the rising air go up even farther. But the higher it rises, the cooler it gets. Finally, when it is cool enough, the condensing vapor forms ice crystals instead of liquid water. The ice crystals begin to collect water droplets to form big drops of water heavy enough to fall to the ground. This starts the rain that comes with a tornado and surrounds the funnel.

The raindrops don't find it easy falling to the ground. The current of air flowing up in and near the funnel blows against them and pushes them right back up. Outside the funnel, where the current is weakest, the heaviest drops manage to push their way through and reach the ground. Meanwhile the smaller drops are blown to bits by the force of the wind. The wind blows against them so hard that it even knocks electrons right out of them. In this way big electrical charges build up in the cloud. When a charge is high enough, it sends an electric spark crashing through the air. The flash of the spark is *lightning*, and it may be said that the noise of the spark is *thunder*, for the present theory is that the heated air, warmed by the spark, rushes out in all directions to cause the sound.

HAILSTONES

Some of the drops of water in a tornado cloud are blown up so high they reach air that is cold enough to freeze them. Then they fall again as little balls of

112

ice. But even a ball of ice has trouble pushing its way through a wind that blows up with great force. It may be blown up again and again. Each time it goes up it has a chance to pick up more moisture in the cloud, so a new layer of ice forms like a shell around the ball. Finally it becomes so heavy that the wind can't hold it back, and it falls to the ground. Hailstones as big as marbles are not unusual in a tornado. If you cut open a hailstone you can see separate layers of ice, one inside the other. If you count these layers, you can find out how many times the hailstone was blown back up in the cloud before it finally became heavy enough to reach the ground.

SIX TORNADOES STRIKE

On June 8, 1953, six tornadoes struck, one after the other, in southern Michigan and northwest Ohio. As they roared across the ground they killed one hundred and thirty-nine people, injured one thousand, and destroyed property worth fifteen million dollars. The greatest destruction was in the city of Flint, where the tornadoes mowed down a row of forty houses and killed one hundred and thirteen people. The number of people injured was so great the hospitals couldn't handle them all. Emergency hospitals were set up in factories and city buildings. This tornado storm was the tenth most costly in the history of the United States.

ECHO IN MASSACHUSETTS

The next day a tornado tore through central Massachusetts, killing ninety-two people and injuring eight hundred. Eight thousand people were left homeless, and property damage was fifty-nine million dollars. After the storm, automobiles were found flattened as though they had been crushed by a giant press. This was the worst tornado to hit New England in seventy-five years.

OPERATION TORNADO

It is an old American custom for people to help each other when they have a big job to do. When the pioneers were moving west and carving farms out of the wilderness, they used to help each other clear the land to prepare it for the plow. Then, when a farmer was ready to build a barn, all his neighbors came to join in the work of "barn-raising." This spirit of good-neighborliness was revived in the city of Flint as a result of the tragedy of June 8, 1953.

After the city had buried its dead, it turned to the problem of rebuilding the wrecked homes for the living. The way in which this was done is an inspiring example of community co-operation. On August 29, 1953, fifty-five hundred men, women and boys turned out as volunteers for "Operation Tornado." Brought together by trade unions, business organizations, churches and the city government, they built one hundred and ninety-three houses that day to replace those destroyed or damaged on June eighth. The owners of the houses supplied the materials, purchased with insurance money or loans. Businessmen supplied tools and trucks free of charge. The workers put in eighty thousand man-hours of voluntary labor. Work proceeded at a brisk pace even though the temperature that day was over ninety degrees. When the job was completed, the people celebrated with a big dance in the open air.

HARNESSING THE WEATHER

Every year there are hurricanes and tornadoes, and every year they kill people and destroy property. When one of these violent storms arises, there is nothing we can do to stop it. The best we can do is try to get out of its way, if we are warned in time. To be able to warn us, the Weather Bureau studies the weather and tries to figure out how it will change.

As the weather men continue to study the weather, they learn more and more about it. The more they learn about it, the better they understand it. And the better they understand it, the more accurately they can predict its changes. But understanding the weather has already taken us a step farther than prediction. It has opened the door to *control* of the weather in the future.

The great American humorist Mark Twain once said: "Everybody talks about the weather, but nobody does anything about it." This isn't true any more. We now know enough about the weather to be able to change it sometimes. Scientific rainmakers are trying to increase the amount of rainfall by "seeding" the clouds at the proper time. They drop dry ice crystals into the clouds and introduce silver-iodide crystals from below. These crystals start the formation of ice crystals, and the ice crystals start the rain.

Cloud seeding is only the first feeble step toward controlling the weather. But it presents us with a great challenge. If we can control rain, can we also learn to control storms? Will the day ever come when we can make storms start and stop when we want them to? Will we be able to make them follow paths that we choose for them? Hurricanes and tornadoes have tremendous power in them. Will we ever be able to harness this power and put it to work for us? Can we take the winds that now destroy people and property, and use them to run giant turbines to generate electricity? The scientists of today turn these questions over to future generations. All of you who read this book will have a share in working out the answers.

APPENDIX:

THE BEAUFORT SCALE
OF WIND FORCE

On a weather map, each weather station is shown by a small circle. Little arrows are attached to the circle to show the direction and force of the wind. The arrow is placed so that it "flies with the wind" and shows its direction in this way. The diagram shows how the arrows would be drawn for an east wind, a west wind, a south wind and a southwest wind.

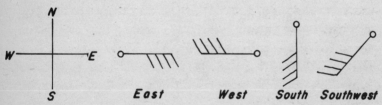

East   West   South Southwest

The strength of the wind is shown by the "feathers" on the arrow. They represent numbers in a special scale of wind force first introduced in 1906, in the English Navy, by Admiral Francis Beaufort. Each full feather stands for 2, and each half-feather stands for 1. By combining the numbers for the feathers, you get the Beaufort number of the wind. The chart that follows shows the meaning of the Beaufort numbers, and how you can recognize the force of the wind without any instruments.

BEAUFORT NUMBER		DESCRIPTION		MILES PER HOUR	TERM USED BY U.S. WEATHER BUREAU
0	○	Calm; smoke rises vertically		Less than 1	Light
1	⌐○	Direction of wind shown by smoke drift, but not by wind vanes		1-3	Light
2	⌐○	Wind felt on face; leaves rustle; ordinary vane moved by wind		4-7	Light
3	⌐○	Leaves and small twigs in constant motion; wind extends light flag		8-12	Gentle
4	⌐○	Raises dust and loose paper; small branches are moved		13-18	Moderate

118

BEAUFORT NUMBER		DESCRIPTION	MILES PER HOUR	TERM USED BY U.S. WEATHER BUREAU
5	\\\o	Small trees in leaf begin to sway; crested wavelets form on inland waters	19-24	Fresh
6	\\\o	Large branches in motion; whistling heard in telegraph wires; umbrellas used with difficulty	25-31	Strong
7	\\\\o	Whole trees in motion; inconvenience felt in walking against wind	32-38	Strong
8	\\\\o	Breaks twigs off trees; generally impedes progress	39-46	Gale

119

BEAUFORT NUMBER	DESCRIPTION		MILES PER HOUR	TERM USED BY U.S. WEATHER BUREAU
9	Slight structural damage occurs (chimney pots and slate removed)		47-54	Gale
10	Seldom experienced inland; trees uprooted; considerable structural damage occurs		55-63	Whole gale
11	Very rarely experienced; accompanied by widespread damage		64-75	Whole gale
12			Above 75	Hurricane

INDEX